Brinner Winners: 60 Super #Delish Breakfast for Dinner Recipes

RHONDA BELLE

ISBN-13: 978-1539462866

ISBN-10: 1539462862

DEDICATION

To Foodies Everywhere...Enjoy & Be Well!

ACKNOWLEDGEMENTS

To the love of my life, Johnny.
You are Mommy's greatest inspiration.

To Mom & Dad (Sunset February 2016).
Love you always...

MOVE OVER BRUNCH, IT'S "BRINNER" TIME!

Who said that the wonderfully comforting taste of bacon, eggs, waffles, or scrumptious hash browns can't also be enjoyed at the end of a long day? This recipe book offers 60 super delish (and super fun) brinner ideas that will please your brood at supper time and even help you save money and time. Try fresh and light soufflés, breakfast pizza or burritos, tempting biscuit creations, mouthwatering pancakes, and more! Go on and indulge...breakfast for dinner, it's a real winner!

Amish Waffles

¾ teaspoon vanilla extract
1 ¾ teaspoon baking powder
1 1/3 whole eggs, well beaten
1 cup milk
2/3 cup all-purpose flour
2/3 cup sifted cake flour
3 ½ tablespoon butter or margarine
Topping:
1¼ teaspoons white corn syrup
1 cup water
2 pinches red food coloring
2/3 whole (3 ounces) raspberry flavored gelatin
4 teaspoons cornstarch
5 ¼ ounces frozen blueberries, defrosted
5 ¼ ounces frozen raspberries, defrosted
7 tablespoons sugar
Vanilla ice cream, optional

For topping: combine water, sugar, corn syrup, food coloring and cornstarch in saucepan; cook over medium heat until thickened. Remove from heat; add gelatin and stir until fully dissolved. Continue cooking and add berries. Keep warm. For waffles: Mix batter ingredients together in order just until smooth. Bake in waffle iron according to manufacturer's directions. Serve warm topping over hot waffles. #Delish!

Apple Pancakes

¼ cup sugar
¼ teaspoon nutmeg
½ teaspoon salt
1½ cup buttermilk
1½ teaspoons cinnamon
1 teaspoon baking powder
1 teaspoon vanilla
2 cups flour
2 eggs, beaten
3 medium apples, peeled and coarsely chopped/grated
Juice from half of a lemon, squeezed
Pinch of cloves

In a large bowl, whisk together the eggs, buttermilk, vanilla and lemon juice. In a separate bowl, whisk flour, baking powder, salt, sugar, cinnamon, nutmeg and cloves. Next, add the dry ingredients to the wet ingredients and stir in chopped apples. Heat a large pan over medium heat and using a ¼ cup, scoop out batter and pour it into the pan into a nice size puddle. Cook until the edges have firmed up and it is a nice golden brown. Flip and repeat on the other side. Serve hot! #Delish!

Bacon & Cheese French Bread

1 (16 ounce) loaf of unsliced French bread
5 slices bacon, cooked and crumbled
2 cups (8 ounces) shredded mozzarella cheese
¼ cup butter or margarine, melted

Cut bread into 1 inch slices. Place sliced bread on a large piece of aluminum foil. Combine bacon and cheese; place between bread slices. Drizzle butter over loaf, and wrap in foil. Bake at 350 degrees for 20 minutes or until thoroughly heated. Enjoy!

Baked Oatmeal

¼ cup chopped nuts and or seeds
¼ cup unsweetened applesauce
½ cup brown sugar, lightly packed
½ teaspoon flaky kosher salt
1½ cups milk
1 cups fresh fruit
1 large egg
1 teaspoons aluminum-free baking powder
2 cups old-fashioned oats
2 tablespoons unsalted butter, melted

Preheat oven to 375 degrees. Melt butter in a medium sized bowl, and set aside to cool to room temperature. In another bowl, mix together oats, brown sugar, nuts/seeds, baking powder, and salt. Into the cooled butter, whisk together milk, applesauce, and egg. Add milk mixture to oat mixture and stir well. Stir in fruit. Pour mixture into a greased baking dish and bake for 20 minutes or until done. Serve warm and enjoy!

Baked Spanish Eggs

½ teaspoon cumin
½ teaspoon dried oregano
1 medium green pepper, diced
1 ounce can of mild green chilies, chopped
2 - 3 tablespoons fresh cilantro or parsley, minced
2 fresh garlic cloves, minced
2 medium tomatoes, diced
2 medium yellow onions, quartered and sliced very thin
2 tablespoons olive oil
3 corn tortillas, cut into squares
3 tablespoons low-fat milk
6 eggs, well beaten
Salt and freshly ground pepper to taste

Preheat the oven to 350 degrees. Heat a large skillet. Toast the cut tortillas on the dry skillet over moderate heat, stirring until crisp. Transfer to a plate to cool. Next, heat the oil in the same skillet. Add the onions and sauté until translucent. Add garlic and pepper and sauté until peppers soften. Add the tomatoes and sauté for another 2 to 3 minutes, just enough to soften. Combine the beaten eggs with the milk in a mixing bowl and stir in the skillet mixture, tortilla bits, and all remaining ingredients. Oil two 9-inch pie pans and divide the mixture among them. Bake for 25 to 30 minutes, or until set and tops turn golden. Let stand for 10 minutes and then cut into wedges to serve. #Delish!

Big Blue Baco-Potatoes

⅛ teaspoon pepper
¼ cup (1 ounce) crumbled blue cheese
¼ cup butter or margarine
¼ cup milk
¼ teaspoon salt
½ cup sour cream
4 medium baking potatoes (about 1½ pounds)
4 slices of bacon

Place bacon slices on a rack in a baking dish; cover with paper towels. Microwave on high for 3 ½ to 4 ½ minutes or until crisp. Drain and crumble; set aside. Scrub potatoes; prick several times with a fork. Place potatoes 1 inch apart on a microwave-safe rack or paper towels. Microwave on high for 10 to 13 minutes, turning and rearranging once; let stand two minutes. Cut a 1 inch lengthwise strip from the top of each potato. Carefully scoop out potato pulp, leaving a ¼ inch shell intact; mash pulp. Combine potato pulp, sour cream, blue cheese, milk, butter, salt and pepper. Spoon potato mixture into shells. Place on a microwave-safe plate. Microwave on high for 2 minutes or until thoroughly heated. Sprinkle with crumbled bacon. #Delish!

Blue Buckwheat Pancakes

½ cup green onions, shredded
1 cup buckwheat flour
1 cup milk
1 tablespoons baking powder
2 tablespoons maple syrup
2 tablespoons melted butter
5 strips of bacon
Blue cheese, cut in small pieces
Maple syrup for serving
Olive oil for frying
Pinch of salt

Place flour, baking powder, salt, milk, butter and maple syrup in a bowl and mix until well combined. Add onion and blue cheese and fry all over a medium heat on a frying pan with a bit of an olive oil. Meanwhile, place bacon in an oven and cook until crispy. Drain and top each pancake with bacon followed by warm maple syrup. #Delish!

Blueberry Lemonzest Pancakes

¼ teaspoon salt
½ teaspoon vanilla
1 cup heaping blueberries
1½ cup cake flour
1 tablespoon (additional) cake flour
1 heaping tablespoon baking powder
1 whole large egg
1 whole lemon, juiced
1½ cup evaporated milk
2 tablespoons butter, melted
3 tablespoons sugar
Extra butter
Maple or pancake syrup
Zest from 1 fresh lemon

Heat a heavy skillet over medium low heat. In a bowl, mix flour, salt, baking powder, and sugar and set aside. In a separate bowl, mix evaporated milk, lemon juice, and lemon zest. Allow to sit for five minutes, and then add egg, vanilla, and melted butter. Mix well.   Pour wet mixture into dry ingredients. Stir gently to incorporate. *Splash in extra evaporated milk if mixture is overly thick.* Next, stir in blueberries. Melt butter in heated skillet. Drop batter ¼ cup at a time into hot butter in pan, and fry pancakes on both sides until golden. Serve with softened butter and warm syrup. #Delish!

Bodacious Breakfast Pizza

1½ cups shredded mozzarella cheese
1 small onion, chopped
1 tube of refrigerator pizza dough (or batch of homemade pizza dough)
2 scallions, sliced
3 whole eggs
4 slices turkey bacon, crumbled (or meat of your choice)
Salt and pepper

Preheat oven to 400 degrees. Unroll pizza dough onto a pizza pan. Top with mozzarella cheese, bacon, onion, and scallions. Clear away toppings slightly in three areas to make room for the eggs. Crack eggs directly onto pizza. Season with salt and pepper. Rearrange toppings, if desired, to cover eggs. Bake for 10 to 12 minutes, or until pizza is lightly browned and eggs are cooked to your preference. Simple & #Delish!

Bountiful Breakfast Pizza

1 cup of tater tots, fried or baked
1 lb. store-bought pizza dough
2 tablespoons olive oil
3 large eggs
3 slices Canadian bacon, cut into small pieces
4 slices of thick Applewood smoked bacon, cooked and cut into small pieces
5 slices of provolone cheese
Fresh chives, minced
Fresh thyme leaves, minced
Salt and black pepper to taste

Preheat oven to 450 degrees. Warm dough to room temperature for 30 minutes and prepare pizza ingredients. Cook tater tots and bacon; slice Canadian bacon. Set aside until dough is ready. Add 1½ tablespoons olive oil into a 12-inch cast-iron skillet. Place room temperature pizza dough inside skillet. Pat into a flat disk using the palm of your hand and then stretch dough out from the center, rotating dough in the skillet to form an even 12-inch circle. Use remaining ½ tablespoon of olive oil to coat the top of pizza dough. Place provolone cheese slices on top. Follow with sliced Canadian bacon and smoked bacon. Arrange tater tots in such a way to allow room for cracked eggs. Place skillet over the stove on high heat. Turn up heat and cook for 4 minutes. Be sure to continually check the underside of the dough until lightly golden brown in the color and oil is bubbling a bit. Remove from skillet, crack eggs onto pizza and season with salt and pepper. Place in oven for 8-10 minutes until the cheese is melted and egg whites are well cooked. Let cool slightly in skillet. Cut into slices and enjoy!

Breakfast Bread & Sausage

½ cup warm water
1 cup white sugar
1 teaspoon salt
2 (.25 ounce) packages active dry yeast
2 cups milk, scalded and cooled
2 eggs, beaten
2 tablespoons margarine, melted
3 cups oil for frying
7 cups all-purpose flour

In a large bowl, stir together the scalded milk, sugar, margarine and salt. Then, in a small bowl, stir together the yeast and warm water. Let stand 10 minutes or until foamy. Stir the yeast mixture into the milk mixture. Blend in the eggs. Mix in flour one cup at a time to make a soft dough. Cover bowl and let rise in a warm place until double. Heat about 1-inch of oil in a deep heavy skillet. Shape large handfuls of dough into flat pancakes and let rest for 10 minutes (for yeast). Next, fry them in the hot oil, turning once, until golden brown. Serve hot alongside cooked sausage links or patties of your choosing. Enjoy!

Broccoli-Cheddar Quiche

¾ cup heavy cream
¾ pound broccoli florets, steamed until crisp-tender
1 cup grated sharp cheddar (4 ounces)
1 store-bought single-crust pie dough
1 tablespoon unsalted butter
2 cups medium diced yellow onion
6 large eggs
Coarse salt and ground pepper

Preheat oven to 375 degrees. Bake a store-bought pie crust until edge is dry and light golden, about 20 minutes. Remove parchment and weights. Meanwhile, in a large skillet, melt butter over medium-high heat and add onion, and salt and pepper to taste. Cook until light golden, for about 8 to 10 minutes. In a medium bowl, whisk together eggs and cream. Add onion, broccoli florets, and cheese and season with ½ teaspoon salt and ¼ teaspoon pepper. Whisk together well, pour into crust, and bake until center of quiche is just set, 40 to 45 minutes. Serve warm or at room temperature. #Delish!

Caribbean French Toast

¼ cup whipping cream
½ cup orange juice
½ teaspoon ground cinnamon
1 large egg
2 tablespoons butter or margarine, divided
2 tablespoons sugar
6 (1 inch thick) slices of French bread
Dash of ground nutmeg
Powdered sugar

Combine orange juice, whipping cream, sugar, egg, cinnamon, and nutmeg. Place mixed ingredients into a baking dish. Place bread slices in mixture; turn slices to coat evenly. Let stand 5 minutes or until all liquid is absorbed. Melt 1 tablespoon butter in a large skillet. Add 3 slices bread; cook over medium heat 3 minutes on each side or until golden brown. Remove from pan; keep warm. Repeat procedure with remaining bread slices. Sift sugar over toast; serve with warm maple syrup. #Delish!

Cheesy Bacon Biscuit Bake

½ pound bacon, cooked and crumbled
½ teaspoons pepper
1 cup cheese
1 tablespoons garlic powder
1 teaspoons salt
2 tablespoons oil
2 teaspoons onion powder
3 cans of make-at-home biscuits
6 eggs

Preheat oven to 350 and grease a large baking dish. Whisk eggs and spices in the bottom of dish. Cut biscuits into four pieces (quarters) and fold into the eggs. Next, add crumbled bacon and cheese. Bake for 25 minutes or until biscuits turn golden. Remove, cool and enjoy!

Cheesy Hash Brown Casserole

1 cup sour cream
1 teaspoon garlic powder
1 teaspoon ground mustard
2 cups (8 ounces) shredded cheddar cheese, divided
2 cups milk
3 green onions, sliced
5 slices bacon, cooked crispy and then crumbled
6 large eggs
8 frozen hash brown patties

Place hash brown patties in a single layer in baking dish coated with nonstick cooking spray. Bake in an oven preheated to 450 degrees for 20 minutes or until golden brown; turn patties after 10 minutes. Remove from oven. Let stand for five minutes. Reduce oven temperature to 350 degrees. Next, add sour cream, garlic powder, mustard and pepper; mix well. Stir in bacon, 1½ cup of the cheese and onions. Pour over hash brown patties. Sprinkle with remaining ½ cup cheese. Bake for 40 to 50 minutes or until center is set edges are golden brown. #Delish!

Cheesy Sausage Muffins

¼ cup chopped green onions
¼ pound ground pork sausage, cooked and drained
½ cup (2 ounces) shredded cheddar cheese
1 (3 ounce) package cream cheese, cut into small cubes
1 cup biscuit mix
2 large eggs, lightly beaten
2/3 cup milk

Combine sausage, cream cheese, cheddar cheese, green onions, and biscuit mix in a large bowl; make a well in center of mixture. Combine eggs and milk; add to the sausage mixture, stirring just until moist. Spoon into a greased muffin pan. Fill ¾ full. Bake at 350 degrees for 35 to 40 minutes. Remove from pan and serve hot. #Delish!

Chicken Hash & Eggs

½ teaspoon finely chopped thyme
¾ cup finely chopped onion
1 cup finely chopped green bell pepper
1 large baked potato, peeled and diced (about 2 ½ cups)
2 cups diced or shredded cooked chicken
2 garlic cloves, minced
2 large jalapeños, stemmed, seeded and minced
2 tablespoons extra-virgin olive oil
2 tablespoons unsalted butter
4 large eggs
Freshly grated Parmigiano-Reggiano cheese, for sprinkling
Freshly ground pepper
Kosher salt

Melt butter in olive oil in a cast iron skillet. Add green pepper, onion, jalapeños, garlic, thyme and a substantial pinches of both salt and pepper. Cook over medium heat, stirring occasionally, until softened, about 7 minutes. Stir in potato and chicken and flatten mixture with a spatula. Turn heat up to high until it turns a bit crusty on the bottom, about 5 minutes. Working in sections, turn the hash over and cook until browned on the other side, 3 to 5 minutes. Using the back of a spoon, make 4 depressions in the hash. Carefully crack eggs into the formed wells and season with salt and pepper. Cover and continue cooking over medium heat until the egg whites are just set, about 4 minutes. Sprinkle the hash with grated cheese and serve immediately from skillet. #Delish!

Dirty Rice with Sausage & Peas

½ cup finely chopped bell
½ cup of vegetable broth
½ tablespoon dried parsley
½ teaspoon dried oregano
1 cup finely chopped celery
1 cup finely chopped onion
1 tablespoon Lawry's seasoned salt
1¾ cups long grain rice
2 bay leaves

2 cloves garlic, finely chopped
2 cups frozen black-eyed peas
2½ cups fat free, low-sodium
6 ounces of turkey apple sausage
Dash of black pepper

In a large skillet, combine vegetable broth and bay leaves; bring to a boil. Add rice and black-eyed peas to broth and cover. Reduce heat to simmer until all liquid is absorbed, about 18 to 20 minutes. Remove bay leaves and place cooked rice and peas in a large bowl. Spray a skillet with cooking spray and heat over medium-high heat. Add onion, celery, bell pepper, seasoning, sausage, garlic, parsley, and oregano. Sauté until sausage is thoroughly cooked, about 5 minutes. Combine with rice and black-eyed pea mixture. Serve while hot. #Delish!

Easy Cheesy Casserole

½ teaspoon garlic salt
1 ¼ cups milk
1 cup (4 ounces) shredded cheddar cheese
1 cup (4 ounces) shredded Swiss cheese
1 cup chopped cooked ham
1 cup sliced fresh mushrooms
1 medium onion, chopped
1 tablespoon all-purpose flour
1 tablespoon prepared mustard
2 tablespoons butter or margarine, melted
4 large eggs beaten
4 slices white sandwich bread
Parsley sprigs (optional)

Place bread slices in bottom of a lightly greased 8 inch baking dish; set aside. Sauté onion and mushrooms in butter until tender; spoon over bread. Top with ham. Combine cheeses and flour; sprinkle over ham. Combine milk and eggs, salt and mustard; pour over cheese. Bake at 375 degrees for 35 minutes or until set let stand for 10 minutes before serving. Enjoy!

Egg Dressing

¼ cup sweetened coconut flakes
½ cup chopped plum tomatoes
¾ cup chopped cucumbers (skin on)
1 cup chopped mango
1 tablespoon chopped fresh cilantro
1 tablespoon orange juice
2 tablespoons fresh lime juice
Salt and pepper to taste
Sprinkling of red pepper flakes

In a small skillet coated with non-stick coating, sauté the coconut over medium-low heat in order to toast/brown it lightly. Combine all of the remaining ingredients, seasoning with the salt and pepper to taste. Easy & #Delish!

Eggs in a Nest

1 can corn beef hash
6 eggs
Salt and pepper to taste
Butter or margarine

Make six, 6-inch squares with aluminum foil. Butter each square. Next, make a nest with corn beef hash on each square of foil. *It should be big enough to hold one egg.* Heat nest on foil for 2 minutes in a skillet. Break an egg into the center of the "nest." Add salt and pepper to taste. Add 1 teaspoon water to the skillet and cover. Remove from skillet when eggs are done. #Delish!

Fiesta Grits

¼ cup sliced ripe olives
¼ teaspoon garlic powder
½ cup (2 ounces) shredded cheddar cheese
½ cup quick – cooking grits
¾ pound lean ground beef
1 (1 ¼ ounce) package taco seasoning mix
1½ cups water
1 cup (4 ounces) shredded Monterey Jack cheese, divided
1 large egg, lightly beaten
1/3 cup chopped tomato
2 large eggs, lightly beaten
2 tablespoons milk
3 tablespoons finely chopped green pepper

Bring water and garlic powder to a boil in a large saucepan; reduce heat and cook for 4 minutes, stirring occasionally. Remove from heat. Combine flour and cheddar cheese; stir into grits. Stir 1 egg into mixture until well blended. Spoon mixture into a lightly greased pie plate and press with back of a spoon to form a pie shell; set aside. Brown beef and taco seasoning mix in a large skillet until meat browns, stirring to crumble meat. Drain. Spread meat mixture into pie shell. Top with ¾ cup Monterey Jack cheese, tomato, ripe olives, and green pepper; set aside. Combine 2 eggs and milk and pour over pie. Bake at 375 degrees for 25 minutes. Remove from oven and sprinkle with remaining 1 cup Monterey Jack cheese, and let stand for five minutes before slicing. #Delish!

Fluffy Pancakes with Pineapple Sauce

⅔ cup milk
1 ¼ cup biscuit mix
1 large egg, beaten
1 tablespoon vegetable oil

Place biscuit mix in a bowl; make a well in center. Combine egg, milk, and oil; add biscuit mix, stirring just until dried ingredients are moistened. For each pancake, pour about ¼ cup batter onto a moderately hot and lightly greased griddle. Turn pancakes when tops are covered with bubbles and edges pancakes look cooked.
Pineapple Sauce:
¼ teaspoon ground ginger
1/3 cup sugar

½ tablespoons lemon juice
1 (20 ounce) can unsweetened crushed pineapple, undrained
1 tablespoon tapioca
Combine all ingredients in a medium saucepan; let stand for 5 minutes. Bring to a boil over medium heat; reduce heat and simmer, stirring occasionally, 2 minutes or until thickened. Serve warm over pancakes. #Delish!

Fun & Fruity Crepes
Fruit Topping:
¼ cup brown sugar
½ cup fresh blueberries
2 cups sliced fresh strawberries
Juice of 1 lime
Crepe Ingredients:
¼ teaspoon cinnamon
1 cup low-fat ricotta cheese
2 tablespoons brown sugar
2 teaspoons margarine
6 (6-inch) flour tortillas
Combine brown sugar and lime juice in a small bowl; stir to dissolve sugar. Stir in fruit and set aside. To prepare crepes, combine cheese, brown sugar, and cinnamon in a small bowl. Spoon an even amount of mixture on half of each tortilla; fold over to enclose filling. Melt 1 teaspoon margarine in a large skillet over medium heat. Place 3 of the filled tortillas in the skillet and cook for several minutes on each side until crisp and lightly browned. Repeat with remaining margarine and tortillas. Spoon fruit topping over crepes and serve hot. Enjoy!

Going Green Omelet
1/3 cup green peas
1 tablespoon mint, shredded
1 tablespoon olive oil
1 tablespoon parmesan
1 teaspoon lemon zest
2 tablespoons butter
3 eggs
Goat cheese
Salt and pepper
Place peas in a small pot with salted boiling water and cook for about 1-2 minutes. Drain and place in a bowl with oil, salt, pepper and lemon zest. Next, in another bowl whisk eggs, salt, pepper and parmesan. Heat butter in a pan and pour in the egg mix. Fry over medium heat until done. Place omelet on a plate, spread peas, goat cheese and mint on top and fold over. Enjoy!

Good Day Muffins

½ cup flaked coconut
½ cup milk
½ cup raisins
½ cup sliced almonds
½ cup vegetable oil
½ teaspoon salt
¾ cup sugar
1½ teaspoons ground cinnamon
1½ teaspoons vanilla extract
2 cups all-purpose flour
2 cups carrots; grated
2 cups peeled apples; chopped
2 teaspoons baking soda
3 eggs
Nonstick baking or cooking spray

In a large bowl, combine flour, sugar, baking soda, cinnamon and salt. In another bowl, beat eggs; add oil, milk and vanilla. Mix well, stirring in dry ingredients just until moistened. Fold in the remaining ingredients. Fill greased of paper lined muffin cups ¾ full. Pour into pre-sprayed muffin pan and bake at 375 degrees for 20-25 minutes or until muffins test done. #Delish!

Grilled Baco-Egg-Cheese Sandwiches

1 egg
2 slices any kind of bread
2 slices bacon
Butter
Cheddar cheese, sliced

Fry bacon to a crisp. Drain on paper towels and set aside. Wipe out the pan to fry the egg next. Heat a flat griddle over medium-high heat. Butter one side of each piece of bread. Assemble the sandwich layers as such - cheese, egg and bacon – with buttered sides out. Place the sandwich on the hot griddle to cook first side; flip carefully to cook the other side. Serve right away. #Delish!

Ham & Cheese Flips

½ cup (2 ounces) shredded cheddar cheese
¾ cup diced cooked ham (about 4 ounces)
1 (6 ounce) can refrigerated biscuits
1½ teaspoons butter or margarine, softened
1 teaspoon dried onion flakes
1 teaspoon milk

Combine butter, onion, ham, and cheese in a small bowl; set aside. Separate biscuits, and place on an ungreased baking sheet. Press or roll each biscuit into a 5 inch of oil. Spoon about ½ cup of mixture onto half of each biscuit. Brush edges of biscuits with water; fold dough overfilling, pressing edges with a fork to seal. Make a 1 inch crescent shaped slit on top of each turnover. Brush with milk and bake turnovers at 375 degrees for 15 minutes or until golden. Enjoy!

Ham & Cheese Tart

1 (9 inch) refrigerated pie crust
8 (1 ounce) slices processed American cheese, divided
2 cups finely chopped, cooked lamb
2 cups chopped onion
2 tablespoons butter or margarine, melted
2 large eggs, lightly beaten
½ cup milk
2 tablespoons grated Parmesan cheese
Dash of pepper

Roll piecrust into a 13 inch circle; placed onto a 12 inch pizza pan. Fold edges under, and crimp; prick with a fork. Bake at 425 degrees for 10 minutes; cool arrange six cheese slices, overlapping, on bake crust; sprinkle with cooked ham. Cook onion in butter in a large skillet over medium to a heat, stirring until tender. Remove from heat; stir in any and next three ingredients. Spoon over ham. Cut each of the remaining two cheese slices into 9 squares. Arrange on top. Bake at 425 degrees on lower of oven 15 minutes or until set. Let stand 10 minutes before serving. #Delish!

Ham & Potato Bake

½ cup (2 ounces) shredded cheddar cheese
½ teaspoon ground pepper
1½ cups heavy cream
1 package (10 ounces) frozen broccoli, thawed and squeezed dry with paper towels
10 ounces sugar-baked ham, thinly sliced
2 large baking potatoes, peeled
2 teaspoons coarse salt
6 large eggs

Preheat oven to 350 degrees. Butter a round cake pan and line bottom of pan with a parchment-paper round. In a large bowl, whisk together eggs and cream; season with salt and pepper. Thinly slice potatoes to less than ¼ inch thick and drop into egg mixture. Coat well. Lift potatoes out of egg mixture and arrange half of them in pan. Layer with ham, broccoli, cheese, and remaining potatoes. Pour egg mixture over top, fully submerging potatoes in egg mixture. Cover with foil and bake until potatoes are tender, about 1 hour. Uncover; continue baking until golden and set, 30 to 45 minutes more. Cool for 15 to 20 minutes in pan. Run a knife around edge, and carefully invert onto a plate. Peel off parchment. Reinvert, top side up. Slice with a serrated knife and serve hot. Enjoy!

Happy Hash Casserole

¼ cup chicken stock
½ cup 1% low-fat milk
½ teaspoon freshly ground black pepper, divided
½ teaspoon kosher salt, divided
1½ cups chopped onion
2 cups shredded hash brown potatoes
2 tablespoons thinly sliced fresh basil
3 garlic cloves, minced
3 ounces reduced-fat Swiss cheese, finely chopped
5 cups fresh baby spinach
6 large eggs, lightly beaten
8 center-cut bacon slices
8 ounces sliced shiitake mushroom caps

Preheat oven to 350 degrees. Cook bacon in a large nonstick skillet over medium heat until crisp. Remove bacon from pan; crumble. Increase heat to medium-high. Add onion, mushrooms, and garlic to drippings in pan; sauté for 6 minutes. Add potatoes and stock; cook 6 minutes, stirring frequently. Next, add spinach, basil, ¼ teaspoon salt, and ¼ teaspoon pepper. Cook for 2 minutes or until spinach begins to wilt. Remove from heat and allow to stand for 10 minutes. Next, stir in crumbled bacon as well as cheese. Place mushroom mixture a baking dish (coat with nonstick cooking spray). Combine remaining ¼ teaspoon salt, ¼ teaspoon pepper, milk, and eggs in a medium bowl. Pour egg mixture over mushroom mixture. Bake at 350°F for 28 minutes. Preheat broiler to high; remove dish while broiler preheats. Broil 3 minutes or until top is browned and just set. Let stand 5 minutes. Enjoy!

Happy Yam Skillet (Gluten-Free)

½ cup mozzarella or goat cheese
½ teaspoon smoked paprika or Lawry's Seasoned Salt
1 medium/large sweet potato
4 large eggs
Salt and pepper to taste

Pierce sweet potato with a fork several times and microwave for 8-10 minutes until soft. Preheat broiler to high and place oven rack on to the highest level. Next, slice potato into thin rounds ¼-inch thick (peel or skin as desired). Coat a skillet with nonstick cooking spray and position potato slices into a flat layer. Crack eggs over potatoes and sprinkle with cheese and a bit of paprika. Place skillet under broiler for 3 minutes and allow eggs and cheese to brown. Carefully remove from oven and serve right away. #Delish with ketchup!

Hearty Hash

1½ lb. ground sausage
2 package onion soup mix
4 cups shredded dried hash brown potatoes
6 cups water
Assorted seasonings to taste (Try hot peppers, chili powder, basil, Italian seasonings, etc.)

Brown meat, breaking it up as it cooks. Add the water and soup mix; stir well. Heat to boiling and simmer a few minutes. Add the dry potatoes and stir to mix. Cover the pot and remove from heat for about 10 minutes to allow the potatoes to swell with water. Then, cook about 5-10 minutes more, adding seasonings. Serve hot. #Delish!

Herbed Omelet

¼ cup butter or margarine
¼ teaspoon pepper
¼ teaspoon salt
1 tablespoon finely chopped fresh basil
1 tablespoon finely chopped fresh chives
1 tablespoon finely chopped fresh parsley
6 large eggs
Parsley sprig (optional)

Whisk together ask, salt, and pepper just until blended. Heat a heavy skillet over medium heat. Add butter, and rotate plan to cold. Pour mixture into skillet. As mixture begins to cook, gently lift edges of omelet with a spatula, and tilt pan so that uncooked portion of mixture flows underneath the cooked portion. Garnish with parsley, if desired. Enjoy!

Italian Grits

¼ teaspoon garlic
¾ of regular grits
1 (14 ounce) jar of pizza sauce
1½ pounds lean ground beef
1 large green pepper, and shall
1 medium onion, chopped
1 pound hot bulk pork sausage
1/8 teaspoon pepper
1/8 teaspoon salt
2 ½ cups (10 ounces) shredded cheddar cheese

Brown sausage and ground beef in a large skillet, stirring until it crumbles; drain well. Cook grits according to package directions; spoon into a lightly greased baking dish. Combine pizza sauce and salt, pepper, and garlic. Layer half each pizza sauce, meat, green pepper, onion, and cheese over grits. Repeat, omitting remaining cheese. Cover and bake at 325° for 25 minutes. Add remaining cheese and bake, uncovered, for an additional five minutes.

Mighty Mushroom Quiche

¼ teaspoon dried thyme
¼ teaspoon ground black pepper
¼ teaspoon salt
½ cup shredded low-fat cheddar cheese
½ teaspoon dried mustard
¾ cup nonfat milk
1 clove garlic, finely chopped
1 cup egg substitute
1 teaspoon dried marjoram
1¼ cups sliced mushrooms
1½ teaspoons dried oregano
2 teaspoons dried basil
3 green onions, finely chopped

Preheat oven to 375 degrees. Spray a large skillet with nonstick cooking spray and heat over medium-high heat. Sauté mushrooms, green onions, and garlic until tender, about 5 minutes. Mix in oregano, basil, salt, marjoram, thyme, ground black pepper, and mustard. Cook until liquid is evaporated, about 2 minutes. Let the mushroom mixture cool for about 5 minutes. Next, in a medium bowl, combine egg substitute, milk, and cheese; beat well. Combine batter with mushroom mixture and pour into a pie dish. Bake for 35 to 45 minutes until filling is puffed, set, and starting to brown. Serve while hot. Enjoy!

Oat Bran Waffles

½ cup all-purpose flour
½ cup whole wheat flour
½ teaspoon salt
¾ cup oat bran
1½ cups skim milk
1 egg, beaten
2 egg whites
2 teaspoons baking powder
3 tablespoons vegetable oil
Vegetable cooking spray

Combine oats bran and flours, baking powder and salt in a medium bowl. Combine milk, oil, and egg you'll; add to dry ingredients, stirring just until moist. Beat egg whites at high-speed with an electric mixer until stiff peaks begin to form; gently fold into batter. Coat a waffle iron with cooking spray and allow waffle iron to preheat. Spoon 1½ cups batter onto hot waffle iron; spreading batter to edges. Bake until lightly browned. Repeat procedure with remaining batter. Serve hot with Maple syrup and enjoy!

One Pan Brinner Delight

¼ cup shredded cheese
½ white potato
3 large eggs
3 sausage links
3 tablespoons milk

Dice sausage links and cook until done, setting aside drippings. Dice potato into small hash size pieces, cook in drippings until done (not crispy) and drain. Beat eggs and milk and add to potatoes. Cook to a soft scramble, adding cheese and sausage. Cook until cheese is melted. Enjoy!

Open-Faced Sandwiches

½ cup light cream cheese
½ cup low sugar orange marmalade
1 cup whole alfalfa sprouts
32 Mandarin orange segments
4 whole we English muffins, split and toasted
8 (1 ounce) slices lean Canadian bacon

Spread 1 tablespoon cream cheese on cut side of each muffin half; spread 1 tablespoon orange marmalade over cream cheese. Top with Canadian bacon. Place on a baking sheet and Royal 5 inches from heat for three minutes or until hot. Remove from oven; top each with 2 tablespoons alfalfa sprouts and 4 orange segments. #Delish!

Pancakes with Strawberries

½ cup light sour cream or nonfat vanilla yogurt
½ cup reduced sugar preserves, any flavor
2 cups fat free just-add-water buttermilk pancake mix
3 cups fresh or frozen strawberries

In a large saucepan, mix berries and preserves. Cook over medium heat until slightly thickened, about 5 minutes. Set aside. In a large bowl, combine pancake mix with water according to package directions. Add enough water to make a slightly thin batter. Pour 1/3 cup batter onto hot griddle or into a large nonstick pan, allowing it to spread to about 5 or 6 inches. Cook until edges are dry. Flip over and cook until done. Repeat until all pancakes are cooked. Place 1/4 cup strawberry mixture in the center of each pancake. Roll up and transfer to serving plates. Drizzle each pancake with remaining strawberry mixture. Top each pancake with 1 tablespoon vanilla yogurt. #Delish!

Papaya Ships

1 (11 ounce) can mandarin oranges, drained
1 cup combination of strawberries and blueberries
1 cup low-fat vanilla yogurt
1 kiwifruit, peeled and sliced
1 small banana, peeled and sliced
1 tablespoon honey
2 papayas, rinsed
2 teaspoons chopped fresh mint (optional)

Cut papayas in half lengthwise, scoop out seeds, and place each half in a medium bowl. Place oranges, banana, kiwifruit, and berries in each papaya. Combine yogurt, honey, and mint; mix well. Spoon over fruit before serving. #Delish!

Pecan Waffles with Bacon

½ cup all-purpose flour
¼ cup whole wheat flour
¼ cup cornstarch
½ slightly rounded teaspoon baking powder
¼ slightly rounded teaspoon baking soda
½ teaspoon salt
1/3 cup organic raw pecans, roughly chopped
1 ¼ cup buttermilk
¼ cup extra-virgin olive oil
1 egg
1½ teaspoons turbinado sugar
1 teaspoon vanilla extract
6 or more slices bacon

Preheat waffle iron (ungreased). In a large mixing bowl, combine all-purpose flour, whole wheat flour, cornstarch, baking powder, baking soda, salt, and pecans. Mix well. In a small, separate bowl, combine buttermilk, olive oil, egg, turbinado sugar, and vanilla together and mix well. Pour mixed, wet ingredients into dry mixed ingredients and fork/fold mixture gently until just combined (lumps should still be visible). Let batter site for up to 30 minutes. Ladle batter into center of waffle maker for each waffle, being careful not to overfill. Place cooked waffles on wire rack and tent loosely with aluminum foil to keep warm while you cook the rest. Just before serving, oven cook bacon slices. Once done, place on top of waffles and serve with butter and syrup. #Delish!

Pretty Pizza Frittata

¼ cup broccoli, chopped
¼ cup onion, chopped
2 tablespoons of water
3-4 slices of uncured pepperoni
5 eggs
5-6 tablespoons tomato or marinara sauce
Large handful spinach
Salt and pepper to taste
Sprinkle of mozzarella and parmesan cheese (optional)

Preheat oven to 450 degrees. Whisk eggs and a bit of water in a bowl, adding salt and pepper as needed and set aside. In a hot skillet, sauté broccoli and onion for a few minutes and season with salt and pepper to taste. Before removing, add spinach and sauté for one additional minute. Pour eggs over sautéed veggies and stir. Cove to allow mix to steam for 1-2 minutes. Next, spoon in chosen sauce, sprinkle on cheese and finally add pepperoni. Place skillet under broiler without a lid for 3-5 minutes. Remove carefully and serve immediately. Garnish with crushed red pepper if desired. #Delish!

Quaint Cheese Quiche

¼ cup flour
1 cup cottage cheese
1 teaspoon baking powder
2 cups shredded cheese (cheddar or your choice)
4 tablespoons butter
5 eggs

Optional ingredients for this recipe include small can of Rotel (diced tomatoes/green chilies), fresh herbs, diced ham or bacon, crumbled sausage.

Place butter in a baking dish, place in oven and heat the oven to 400 degrees. While butter melts, whisk eggs in a large bowl. Add flour and baking powder, and whisk until smooth. Fold in cheeses and any optional ingredients. Once butter has completely melted, pour the egg mixture over the melted butter in the pan, and bake for 30 minutes.

Quinoa Bowls

¼ cup flaked unsweetened coconut
½ cup uncooked quinoa
¾ cup light coconut milk
1 cup sliced banana
1 cup sliced strawberries
1 tablespoon light brown sugar
1/8 teaspoon salt
2 tablespoons water

Preheat oven to 400 degrees. Place quinoa in a mesh strainer and sit it in a large bowl. Cover quinoa with water and use your hands to rub the grains together for 30 seconds; rinse and drain quinoa. Repeat the procedure twice. Drain well. Next, combine quinoa, coconut milk, 2 tablespoons water, brown sugar, and salt in a medium saucepan, and bring to a boil. Reduce heat, and simmer 15 minutes or until liquid is absorbed, stirring occasionally. Stir mixture constantly during the last 2 minutes of cooking. While quinoa cooks, spread flaked coconut in a single layer on a baking sheet. Bake at 400°F for 5 minutes or until golden brown. Cool slightly. Next, place about ½ cup quinoa mixture in each of 4 bowls. Top each serving with ¼ cup strawberry slices, ¼, cup banana slices, 1 tablespoon toasted coconut. Serve warm. #Delish!

Rainbow Pepper Omelets

¼ teaspoon ground black pepper
½ teaspoon dried basil
1 red bell pepper, seeded and thinly sliced
1 teaspoon olive oil
1 yellow bell pepper, seeded and thinly sliced
2 teaspoons grated Parmesan cheese
4 egg whites

In a large nonstick pan over medium heat, warm oil; add red and yellow bell peppers and cook, stirring frequently for 4 to 5 minutes. Keep warm over low heat. In a small bowl, lightly whisk together egg whites, basil, and ground black pepper. Coat a small nonstick pan with nonstick cooking spray. Warm over medium-high heat for 1 minute. Add half of the egg mixture, swirling the pan to evenly coat the bottom. Cook for 30 seconds or until the eggs are set. Carefully loosen and flip. Cook for 1 minute or until firm. Sprinkle half of the red and yellow bell peppers over the eggs. Fold to enclose the filling. Transfer to a plate. Sprinkle with 1 teaspoon Parmesan cheese. Repeat with the remaining egg mixture, peppers, and cheese. Enjoy!

Rancher's Breakfast Burrito

½ teaspoon garlic powder
½ teaspoon onion powder
½ teaspoon smoked paprika
1 can black beans, drained and rinsed
1 onion, diced
1 red bell pepper, diced
1 russet potato, peeled and diced
1 sweet potato, peeled and diced
3 – 4 tablespoons of milk or water
8 eggs
8 ounces of fresh mushrooms, quartered
Flour Tortillas
Fresh cilantro
Grated cheese
Olive oil
Pinch cayenne pepper
Salsa
Salt and pepper to taste

In a small bowl, toss potatoes, onion, bell pepper, and mushrooms with garlic powder, onion powder, smoked paprika, cayenne, and a good healthy pinch of salt and pepper. Apply a small drizzle of olive oil and spread out into a single layer on a baking sheet. Roast at 375 degrees for about 30 minutes, or until veggies are tender. Meanwhile, make scrambled eggs (eggs, milk, and salt/pepper) as you normally would until set. Assemble the breakfast burritos by layering roasted vegetables, scrambled eggs, black beans, a little grated cheese, and a little cilantro in the center of the tortilla. Roll it all up and serve with salsa. Enjoy!

Riveting Rice Pudding

¼ cup granulated sugar
¼ teaspoon ground cinnamon
½ cup raisins
1 egg
1 egg white
1/8 teaspoon ground nutmeg
1 1/3 cups 1% low-fat milk
2 tablespoons margarine, melted
2½ cups cooked white rice
5 cups sliced berries of your choice (fresh)
Chopped mangos

Heat oven to 350° degrees and spray a 13 x 9-inch baking dish with nonstick cooking spray. Combine rice, sugar, margarine, milk, eggs, cinnamon, nutmeg, and raisins. Mix well. Pour into baking dish. Bake in oven until top is golden brown, approximately 30 minutes. Top pudding with fruit and enjoy!

Salmon Feast Pancakes

½ ounces plain flour
2 eggs
2 tablespoons milk
3½ ounces tinned salmon, drained and deboned
3½fl ounces double cream
Cooking oil
Dash of baking powder
Handful fresh chives, chopped
Handful fresh dill (optional garnish)
Pinch of salt
Squeeze lemon juice

Mix flour, baking powder, eggs, salt, chives, milk, and fish. Heat a frying pan with cooking oil and fry up the pancakes (1 tablespoon heaps). Flash fry each side for 1-2 minutes. Drain when done. In a small bowl, mix cream and lemon juice. Stir and let sit for 10 minutes to create sour cream. Serve atop each pancake and garnish with dill. #Delish!

Salmon Chowder

¼ teaspoon pepper
½ teaspoon salt
¾ cup chopped onion
1 (15 oz.) can salmon; remove skin & bones, drain, reserve liquid
1 tablespoon bacon drippings
2 cups milk
2 medium sized raw potatoes, cubed
3 tablespoons flour
5 slices bacon

Fry bacon until crisp, drain and crumble. Reserve bacon drippings and use them to sauté onion over medium-low heat until golden brown. Combine flour, salt and pepper. Add to onion mixture, stir. Measure salmon liquid and add water to make 3 cups. Gradually add to onion mixture over medium heat. Transfer onion-liquid mixture to a 3-quart saucepan. Add potatoes; bring mixture to a boil over medium heat. Cover, reducing heat to low and simmer for 20 minutes, stirring occasionally. Add salmon, milk and crumbled bacon. Heat thoroughly for about 8 minutes, stirring occasionally. Serve hot and enjoy!

Sausage Egg & Cheese Simmer

¾ cup heavy cream
1 ¼ cups whole milk
1½ cups shredded cheddar cheese
1 lb. breakfast sausage
1 teaspoon black pepper
1 teaspoon salt
7 eggs
8 frozen buttermilk biscuits, partially thawed and halved

Preheat oven to 375 degrees. Brown the sausage, breaking it into chunks until done. Drain fat and set aside. Next, whisk together the eggs, milk, cream, salt and pepper in a large bowl and set aside. Coat baking dish with cooking spray. Layer in eight of the halved biscuits. Sprinkle half of the cooked sausage over the biscuits followed by a layer of half of the cheese. Add the eight remaining half biscuits and top with the remaining sausage. Then, pour the egg mixture over the top. Crumble all remaining cheese on top of the casserole and bake until eggs have set (center is firm and top is golden), about 10-15 minutes. Remove, cool and serve. Enjoy!

Spinach Omelet

½ onion
3 – 5 medium tomatoes, chopped
Half package of fresh baby spinach
One 16 ounce container of egg whites
Salt and pepper to taste

Chop onion, sauté in large skillet for about 2-3 minutes. Add fresh baby spinach and chopped tomatoes cook for another minute. Add egg whites, salt and pepper, and cover until eggs are cooked. Plate your omelet and sprinkle on some shredded cheese or salsa for extra flavor. Enjoy!

Sunrise Potato Hash

¼ teaspoon pepper
¼ teaspoon salt
1 cup milk or half and half
1 teaspoon chile powder
1 teaspoon ground cumin
1½ cups roasted assorted bell peppers and onions
2 cups shredded Mexican cheese blend
4 cups roasted red potatoes
8 eggs

Preheat oven to 350 degrees. Grease a casserole dish. Place roasted potatoes and onions in bottom of the dish. In a medium bowl, mix eggs, milk or half/half, cumin, chile powder, and salt and pepper. Next, add 1 cup of shredded cheese to the egg mixture and pour over the potatoes. Top with the remaining cheese and bake uncovered for 30 -40 minutes until cheese is browned and eggs are set. Remove, cool slightly and enjoy!

Super Southwestern Omelet

⅛ teaspoon coarse salt
½ cup shredded pepper Jack cheese
1 tablespoon packed fresh cilantro leaves
1 teaspoon olive oil or butter, for pan
2 large eggs
2 tablespoons salsa

In a small bowl, whisk together eggs and salt until well blended and slightly frothy. Add olive oil or butter to a heated pan and pour in egg mixture. As it cooks, fill with cheese, salsa, and cilantro leaves. Fold one half of the cooked egg over the top of the other and flip (take care not to spill your filling). Finish cooking, remove from pan and garnish with additional cheese and/or salsa. Enjoy!

Sweet Potato Hash

¼ cup vegetable oil
1 teaspoon cumin
1 teaspoon red pepper flakes
1 teaspoon salt
2 cups fresh bell peppers and onions, chopped
2 medium sweet potatoes, peeled and cubed

Heat oil in a large skillet over medium-high heat. Sauté bell peppers and onions for 5 minutes or until tender. Add remaining ingredients and reduce heat to medium. Cook for 20 to 25 minutes, stirring every 2 to 3 minutes. Sweet potatoes will begin to stick to the skillet, but continue to stir gently until they cook through. Spoon onto a plate and serve while hot. #Delish!

Taco Touchdown

¼ cup fresh cilantro leaves
¼ cup fresh Pico de Gallo
¼ teaspoon black pepper
½ cup black beans, rinsed and drained
½ cup shredded cheese, Mexican blend
½ ripe peeled avocado, chopped
2 tablespoons Mexican crema
2 teaspoons olive oil
4 (6-inch) corn tortillas
4 large eggs
4 lime wedges

Preheat broiler to high. Arrange tortillas on a baking sheet; lightly coat tortillas with nonstick cooking spray. Broil 2 minutes; remove pan from oven. Turn tortillas over. Top each tortilla with 2 tablespoons cheese and 2 tablespoons beans. Broil 1 minute or until cheese melts. Remove from oven. Heat a large nonstick skillet over medium-high heat. Add oil to pan; swirl to coat. Crack eggs into pan; cook 2 minutes. Cover and cook 2 minutes or until whites are set. Place 1 egg in center of each tortilla; sprinkle with pepper. Top tacos evenly with Pico de Gallo, crema, avocado, and cilantro. Serve with lime. #Delish!

Turkey & Cheese Burritos

¼ cup of pancake syrup
¼ cup of shredded cheese, Mexican blend
10-12 slices of honey smoked turkey breast
5 egg whites, beaten
5 flour tortillas

Heat tortillas in microwave or oven (keep warm). Cut turkey up and heat in skillet. Add egg whites and cook thoroughly. Microwave burritos for 15 seconds and place cooked, scrambled eggs on top. Follow with cheese and syrup. Roll and enjoy!

Turkey Crêpes

½ cup fresh mushrooms, sliced
½ cup fresh mushrooms, sliced
¾ cup (3 ounces) shredded cheddar cheese
1 (4 ounce) jar slice pimiento, drained
1/3 cup chopped celery
1/3 cup chopped onion
1/3 cup grated parmesan cheese
1/3 cup slivered almonds, toasted
2 ½ cups chopped cooked turkey breast
Cherry tomatoes
Crêpes
Vegetable cooking spray
White wine sauce

Sauté mushrooms, onion and celery in a large skillet coated with cooking spray until vegetables are tender. Add turkey, pimiento, and 1 cup white wine sauce, stirring gently. Spoon the mixture down center of the spotty side of each crêpe, dividing mixture equally among crêpes. Fold sides over, and place seem side up in a lightly greased baking dish. Spoon remaining white wine sauce over crêpes. Cover and bake at 350 degrees for 20 minutes. Sprinkle cheese over crêpes; bake, uncovered, an additional 5 minutes. Remove from oven; sprinkle with almonds. Garnish if desired with cherry tomatoes. Enjoy!

Vegetable Brunch Pie

⅛ teaspoon ground cayenne pepper
½ teaspoon garlic powder
½ teaspoon onion powder
½ teaspoon salt
¾ cup baking mix
¾ cup egg substitute
¾ cup shredded low-fat cheddar cheese
1 (8-ounce) package mushrooms, sliced
1 cup low-fat milk
1 medium onion, chopped
1 tablespoon vegetable oil
1 teaspoon brown sugar
2 ¼ cups chopped cauliflower florets
4 ½ cups (about 6 ounces) of mustard, or collard greens, finely chopped

Place an oven rack in the middle of the oven and preheat to 375 degrees. Spray a 10-inch pie dish with nonstick cooking spray and set aside. In a microwave safe bowl, microwave cauliflower on high for
3 minutes, or steam it on the stovetop. Pour vegetable oil into a 12-inch skillet and heat over medium heat. Sauté onion and mushrooms until tender, about 5 minutes. Add greens, garlic powder, onion powder, brown sugar, salt, and cayenne pepper. Sauté for another 3 minutes until greens wilt. Stir the cooked cauliflower into the greens mixture and place in the pie dish. Sprinkle with cheese. In a medium bowl, combine milk, egg substitute, and baking mix. Whisk until well blended and pour over vegetable mixture. Bake 30 to 35 minutes or until golden brown. Serve while hot. #Delish!

Vegetarian Scramble Wraps

¼ cup grated low-fat cheddar cheese
1 cup chopped fresh or frozen vegetables (bell peppers, onions, broccoli, and mushroom mix)
1 cup egg substitute
2 (6-inch) flour tortillas

Spray a medium skillet with nonstick cooking spray and heat over medium heat. Cook vegetables until tender, about 5 minutes. Add egg substitute and stir until thoroughly cooked. Warm tortillas in the microwave for no more than 10 seconds. Pace half of the egg mixture in each tortilla and sprinkle with cheese. Wrap and enjoy!

Thank you for your purchase!
May you enjoy and be well!

ABOUT THE AUTHOR

I am a Tennessee native and a connoisseur of good eats. My culinary delights are inspired by my Southern roots.

I am from cornbread and cabbage, fried chicken and Kool-Aid soaked lemon slices.

I am from hen houses, persimmon trees and juicy, red tomatoes on the vine.

I am from sunflowers growing wild in summer and homemade ice cream in the winter.

I am from family reunions, blue collar men, happy housewives, and Sunday dinners.

I am from spiritual folks who didn't always get it right, but believed in the power of prayer – and taught it to their kids.

I am from the hottest of hot summers and kids running barefoot and free through thirsty Tennessee grass.

I am from a grandmother who sang gospel that was magic...song drenched air would tumble from her lungs, leap into your spirit and make you feel fantastic things.

I am from hard, heartfelt lessons about living and kitchens full of the perfume of love.

♥♥♥ *This book is from my heart to yours.* ♥♥♥

For info, freebies & new book notices, follow @SoDelishDish on social media!
Scan with your smartphone!

FIND MORE BOOKS ONLINE

CPSIA information can be obtained
at www.ICGtesting.com
Printed in the USA
LVHW061652261122
734075LV00011B/989